Dwight D. Eisenhower

☆ ☆ ☆

Dwight D. Eisenhower

Michael J. Birkner

AMERICA'S

34TH

PRESIDENT

Children's Press®
A Division of Scholastic Inc.
New York / Toronto / London / Auckland / Sydney
Mexico City / New Delhi / Hong Kong
Danbury, Connecticut

Library of Congress Cataloging-in-Publication Data

Birkner, Michael J., 1950–
    Dwight D. Eisenhower / Michael J. Birkner.
        p. cm. — (Encyclopedia of presidents. Second series)
Includes bibliographical references and index.
 ISBN 0-516-22969-9
  1. Eisenhower, Dwight D. (Dwight David), 1890–1969—Juvenile literature.
2. Presidents—United States—Biography—Juvenile literature. I. Title.
II. Series: Encyclopedia of presidents (2003)
E836.B54 2005
973.921'092—dc22   2004020391

CHILDREN'S PRESS and associated logos are trademarks and or registered
trademarks of Scholastic Library Publishing. SCHOLASTIC and associated
logos are trademarks and or registered trademarks of Scholastic Inc.
1 2 3 4 5 6 7 8 9 10 R 14 13 12 11 10 09 08 07 06 05

Contents

Chapter 1

"OK, Let's Go"

On the evening of June 5, 1944, General Dwight D. Eisenhower, supreme commander of Allied forces in Europe, met with his officers in southern England. He paced the room, his head down, hands clasped behind his back. He was about to launch the greatest military invasion the world has ever seen. The outcome of the attack would affect the course of the world for years to come. The German army had overrun most of Europe. The countries united against Germany, known as the Allies, had begun to wear down the powerful German military machine. To win, however, they needed to attack the Germans in heavily defended France.

The attack had to be made by sea. It would mean facing German defenders on beaches strewn with booby traps and explosive mines, then unloading thousands of men and millions of tons of heavy military equipment to begin a land offensive. The Allied invasion would test the will and the abilities of troops from the United States, Great Britain, Canada, Australia, and elsewhere.

The planners chose to attack across the stormy English Channel against the beaches of the French region called Normandy. As the day for the invasion approached, the weather was terrible, with slashing rain and high winds. Unless conditions improved, Allied airplanes would not be able to fly, nor would the thousands of ships and landing craft be able to deliver the needed soldiers and supplies.

Eisenhower postponed the invasion for 24 hours because of the weather. Some of his advisers said "go" and others said "wait," but the final decision was his alone. After receiving a little encouraging news from his top weather expert, he said, "I am quite positive that the order must be given." Nearly 7,000 ships of every description began their journey toward the French coast, but as the night wore on, the rains and winds grew worse. Eisenhower knew he could still call off the invasion. After one more meeting with his top officers just before dawn, he said quietly, "OK, let's go."

The date for the invasion was June 6, 1944, known to the participants as D-Day. In the tense days after those first landings, it became clear that the great invasion was a success. Allied forces were soon driving the German army back.

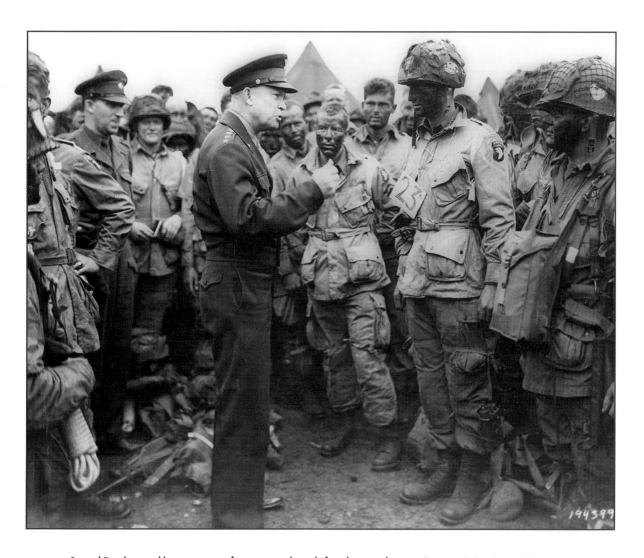

General Eisenhower addresses a group of paratroopers hours before they parachute into France on D-Day, June 6, 1944.

In less than a year, Germany would surrender, ending the war in Europe. Dwight Eisenhower went on to win other battles and fill other important positions of leadership. Within nine years he would be the 34th president of the United States. Yet the great D-Day invasion would always seem the high point of his life.

Growing Up in the Heartland of America ——

He was born David Dwight Eisenhower on October 14, 1890, in Denison, Texas. His father and mother, David and Ida, had met in college in Kansas and married in 1885. David Dwight was their third son. In later years, the family grew to include six sons (a seventh died in infancy). When David Dwight was a boy, his mother reversed his two given names to avoid confusion between him and his father. He used that name order for the rest of his life.

The Eisenhower family had German and Swiss roots. The first Eisenhowers to reach North America arrived in southeast Pennsylvania in the 1700s and farmed there for generations. In about 1878, Dwight's grandfather Jacob moved his family to Kansas to take up wheat farming near Abilene. David, Dwight's father, was about 15 years old at the time of the move. David farmed in Kansas and tried his hand at running a store. When the store failed, he found a railroad job in Texas, where Dwight was born. In 1892 before Dwight turned two years old, the Eisenhower family moved back to Abilene, where Dwight would spend his boyhood.

The Eisenhowers were a lively family. They never got rich, but they never felt poor. The boys had food enough to eat, beds to sleep in, and loving but strict parents. "If we were poor, we were unaware of it," Dwight later remembered. David Eisenhower was the disciplinarian. He did not hesitate to use a strap when

The Eisenhower Name

The name Eisenhower means "ironworker" in German, suggesting that in the distant past, the family trade was in iron mining or in creating iron implements.

☆☆☆

he though the occasion called for it. Once, when he was punishing Dwight's older brother Edgar, Dwight interrupted the punishment. "I don't think anyone ought to be whipped like that," he said, "not even a dog." His father said nothing, but he stopped the whipping.

Ida Eisenhower was the major influence on her sons. Strongly religious, she had the children take turns reading the Bible out loud during their childhood years. Ida emphasized the importance of hard work and self-reliance. She assigned chores to each boy, and taught them life skills, including cooking.

Dwight was bright and curious, with blond hair and a winning smile, but he could be difficult. When things went wrong, he often lost his temper. When he was ten years old, Dwight was not allowed to go trick-or-treating with his older brothers on Halloween. He was so angry that he went out to an old apple tree near his house and began smashing his fists into the tree. David Eisenhower sent his son to bed after a whipping. Then Ida came into the room. After sitting with

The Eisenhower family in 1902. Dwight David is at the far left. He is 11 or 12 years old.

Dwight for a while, she told him that he had only hurt himself. She quoted the Bible: "He that conquereth his own soul is greater than he who taketh a city." Dwight never fully overcame his temper, but he learned to keep it in check most of the time. Those who knew him best were amazed by his self-discipline.

Life in a Pioneer Town

As a small boy, Ike roughhoused with his brother Ed, and got drawn into his share of schoolyard battles. His parents did not approve of fighting, but his father made clear to his sons that if a bully was picking on them, they should fight back. Dwight did not need much encouragement to do that. When he came home with a black eye, it disturbed his mother, who opposed violence and fighting in any form.

Despite his temper, young Dwight easily made friends, and they soon gave him the nickname that would follow him through life—"Ike." He enjoyed schoolyard games, and later went hunting and fishing with his friends. In winter he loved to go skating and sledding. Sometimes he even hooked his sled behind a horse. He later recalled that the rider, "lying on his belly, took a fair amount of snow from the horse's hoofs." Most of all, he loved sports—especially baseball and football.

In school, Ike proved to be a good student. He enjoyed reading history, especially the exploits of great military heroes. One of his favorites was Hannibal, the ancient general who surprised his Roman enemies by crossing the Italian Alps on elephants. Ike also enjoyed math. He was so good in geometry that his teachers made him work out one geometric proof after another without using the textbook. He enjoyed this and mastered the subject.

Eisenhower's boyhood home in Abilene, Kansas. Today it is a part of the Eisenhower Center, which includes the presidential library, a museum, and his burial place.

Ike's life in Kansas was filled with hard labor. During his high school years, he found a variety of ways to make extra money. He raised sweet corn and cucumbers in the family garden, picked apples each fall at a local orchard, helped harvest wheat, and worked in an ice plant. Through his career, he was well known for welcoming assignments that required hard work.

Planning for College

It was always assumed the Eisenhower boys would get a college education, but there was too little money to pay tuition for all of them. Ike and his older brother Edgar hatched a plan to support each other through college. First Ike would stay home and work to help pay Edgar's expenses at college. Then Edgar would return to Abilene and enable Ike to attend college. The plan got off to a good start. Edgar attended the University of Michigan. For two years after high school, Ike stayed in Abilene, working different jobs to help his brother.

By then, Edgar was well established in at Michigan. He would graduate and pursue a career as a lawyer. At the same time, Ike had found a way to continue his education without his brother's financial help. In the fall of 1910, he and his good friend Everett "Swede" Hazlett applied both to the U.S. Naval Academy and the U.S. Military Academy. Ike passed the demanding entrance exams and was hoping for an appointment to the naval academy. He learned, however, that he would be too old (nearly 21) to begin study at the academy. Fortunately, the military academy's age requirements were not so strict, and after further tests, Ike gained an appointment there.

Ike was overjoyed, and he looked forward to beginning his studies in the summer of 1911. His mother was less enthusiastic. As a *pacifist* who opposed wars of any kind, it hurt her to see her son go off to a military academy. She accepted his decision, but after she saw him off on his trip to the academy, she went to her room and cried. Milton Eisenhower wrote that it was the first time he ever heard his mother weep.

West Point

The military academy was located at West Point, New York, about 60 miles (96 kilometers) north of New York City. It had been the leading training ground for future army officers since the early 1800s. The academy had a strong sense of tradition and pride. From his early days at West Point, Ike knew he had come to the right place. He later wrote that when he raised his right hand to take his oath as a cadet, "a feeling came over me that the expression 'The United States of America' would now mean something different than it ever had before. From here on it would be the nation I would be serving, not myself."

The "plebes," as first year students were known, were forced to obey the orders of any upperclassman. Ike remembered that they were "shouted at all day long by self-important upperclassmen, telling us to run here and run there; pick up our clothes; bring in that bedding; put our shoulders back, keep our eyes up, and keep running, running, running." Ike accepted this hazing without complaint. When he became an upperclassman, however, he was reluctant to treat the new plebes in the same fashion.

West Point

During the Revolutionary War, West Point, New York, was an important military outpost on the Hudson River between New York City and Albany. Later it became the site of the U.S. Military Academy, where the future leaders of the United States Army received their early training. Graduates included Robert E. Lee, who served as superintendent of the academy and later as the leading Confederate general in the Civil War; Ulysses S. Grant, the victorious Union general in that war who later served as president; John J. Pershing, the U.S. commander during World War I; and many others.

★ ★ ☆

As a student, Ike did not work especially hard, nor did he win many honors. His main interest in college was not studies, but sports, especially football. Although he was not a big man—during his first year he weighed only about 150 pounds (68 kilograms)—he was fast on his feet, and a strong player. By his second year he had gained enough weight to make the varsity squad. "I was still light for line-plunging and linebacking," he recalled, "but my enthusiasm made up somewhat for my lack of tonnage."

During his sophomore year, Ike's love for football almost ended his army career. Earlier, he had injured his knee in a horseback-riding accident. Then, near the end of the football season, he damaged the knee further. The painful injury

Cadet Dwight Eisenhower during his last year at the U.S. Military Academy.

ended his days as a football player. Unless it healed properly, it could even keep him from receiving a commission as an army officer after graduation.

Unable to play football, he became a cheerleader for a time and coached the junior varsity football squad. He accumulated demerits for minor infractions, like messiness, showing up late to breakfast, and "dancing improperly." By the time he graduated in 1915, he stood 125th of 162 in the class in discipline. He also was not an outstanding student. Still, he graduated from West Point in good standing. Best of all, he had made many friends, men with whom he would serve in peace and war for many years to come.

As Ike and his class left the academy in 1915, a major war had begun between the nations of Europe. It seemed possible that the United States would become involved. Like his classmates, Dwight Eisenhower hoped that it might provide an early opportunity to serve his country.

Chapter 2

First Assignment

Ike's career as a military officer did not begin as he had hoped. He wanted a posting to the Philippine Islands, then a United States territory, halfway around the world in Asia. He was looking forward to seeing faraway places. Instead, he was sent to the 19th Infantry Regiment at Fort Sam Houston, near San Antonio, Texas. It was an out-of-the-way assignment to a hot, dusty base, but Eisenhower accepted it without complaint.

Ike's duties proved to be light. He had time to coach a local football team to earn extra money, go hunting, and play poker with friends. He also fell in love. The object of his affection was a 19-year-old Colorado girl named Mamie Doud, who was visiting San Antonio with her family. "Mamie attracted my eye instantly," Ike later recalled. She was "a vivacious and attractive girl, smaller than average, saucy in the look about her face and in her whole attitude."

Mamie Doud at about the time she met Eisenhower. They were married in 1916.

For her part, Mamie Doud liked Ike. "He's just about the handsomest male I have ever seen," she told a friend. When Ike asked her to join him as he walked his rounds, she quickly accepted. They soon began to date. On Valentine's Day, 1916, Ike proposed marriage and Mamie accepted. Her parents quickly gave their consent, and on July 1, 1916, Mamie and Ike were married at the Doud home in Denver, Colorado. Soon afterward they traveled to Abilene to meet Ike's parents. His parents and his brothers quickly agreed that Mamie was the right partner for Ike.

Military life was difficult for the young couple. In the next few years, Ike was stationed at more than a dozen bases. Sometimes Mamie traveled with him, but often they were separated for months at a time. When there was no housing for married officers, Mamie lived with her parents in Denver or San Antonio. As Ike's career progressed, Mamie gradually learned to accept their unpredictable life. When they were together, the Eisenhowers became the center of a lively social life with other young army families. They entertained so frequently that their residence was known as Club Eisenhower.

Not Going to War

In the summer of 1917, the United States declared war on Germany and entered the Great War (now known as World War I). It began a crash program to train ground troops for the fighting in Europe. Like other young officers, Ike hoped for an assignment to combat overseas, but it never came. Instead, he was assigned to training camps in Georgia and Maryland, then to a tank training camp in Gettysburg, Pennsylvania. Once again, he swallowed his disappointment and did the best job he could.

At Camp Colt, in Gettysburg, Pennsylvania, Eisenhower helped develop tactics for a new and untested weapon—the

Fast Facts

WORLD WAR I

Who: The Central powers (Germany, Austria-Hungary, Turkey, and others) against the Allied powers (Great Britain, France, Russia, Italy, and others)

When: August 1, 1914, to November 11, 1918

Why: Long-standing rivalries for power and territory in Europe began the war; the U.S. entered in 1917 to support the Allied powers.

Where: In Europe, the Middle East, and Africa; and on the Atlantic Ocean

Outcome: Armistice was signed on November 11, 1918. The Treaty of Versailles, approved June 1919, took territory from Germany, broke up Austria-Hungary, required Germany to pay heavy *reparations* (money damages) to France and Britain, and established the League of Nations to prevent future wars.

During World War I, Eisenhower commanded 6,000 men at Camp Colt, a tank training center in Gettysburg, Pennsylvania.

motorized tank. During his months there, he trained hundreds of tank operators, many of whom saw service in France during 1918. Ike worked hard to prepare his recruits for combat. Many were poorly prepared for military service, but he trained them as well as possible in the brief time he had with them.

Even as the training proceeded, Eisenhower was faced with an even greater challenge. Cases of Spanish *influenza* (a killer form of the flu) were first identified at Fort Riley, an army base in Kansas. During 1918 and early 1919, it would kill nearly 800,000 Americans, many of them young adults. When the influenza appeared at Camp Colt, Ike acted quickly to quarantine the sick men and to set up makeshift hospitals for hundreds. He gained experience in dealing with local political leaders, local residents, and the army chain of command. By taking decisive action during the epidemic, he saved many lives. His performance was later commended by his superiors.

In Ike's free hours in Gettysburg, he and Mamie enjoyed small town life with their little boy Doud, or "Icky," as he was known to all. Born in 1917, Icky was adored by his parents and was a favorite of the troops. The Eisenhowers entertained officers and townspeople at their home near the Gettysburg College campus. They also studied the great Civil War battle that had raged in and around the town for three days in 1863. The Eisenhowers found Gettysburg much to their liking. More than 30 years later, when they had the opportunity to settle down, they purchased a farm in Gettysburg.

The Great Convoy ──────────────

Late in 1918, Germany agreed to an armistice ending the fighting in the Great War. Soon the tank training school at Camp Colt began closing down its operations. Early the next year, Ike heard that the army was planning a great *convoy* (a group of heavy military vehicles) to travel from Washington, D.C., to San Francisco. The convoy was designed to test the army's ability to move across the United States in case of a national emergency. Ike thought that the trip sounded like a great adventure and volunteered to serve in it. The convoy left Washington on July 7, 1919. In the next weeks, Ike would see America as he had never seen it before.

The highways of 1919 ranged in quality from "average to nonexistent," according to one participant in the convoy. Most were unimproved dirt or gravel roads. The army's heavy vehicles averaged just over 50 miles (80 km) per day, and finally arrived in San Francisco on September 6, after 62 days. The troops had to stop constantly to deal with breakdowns, vehicles stuck in the mud, and accidents. There was plenty of time for sightseeing, too. The experience affected Eisenhower deeply. He knew that America needed better roads if it was to meet its needs for commerce and national security. Years later as president, he would do something about this.

Heartbreak and Happiness ————————

In December 1920, Icky came down with scarlet fever, then a dangerous childhood disease. On January 2, 1921, he died. He was only three years old. The Eisenhowers were "completely crushed," Ike later remembered. It was, he said, the "greatest disaster" of his life, and neither Ike nor Mamie ever really got over

Lieutenant and Mrs. Dwight Eisenhower early in their marriage.

it. Every year for the rest of his life, Ike sent Mamie flowers on September 24, Icky's birthday.

Happiness returned to the Eisenhower family in 1922, when Mamie gave birth to another son, John Sheldon Doud Eisenhower. Not surprisingly, the Eisenhowers tended to spoil their son, but Ike also set high standards for him. John followed his father to West Point and made his own way as an army officer, a diplomat, and a popular historian.

Seeing America and the World

At the end of World War I, the citizens and the government of the United States were eager to forget about wartime. Congress slashed budgets for military spending, and the size of the army shrank rapidly. This left fewer opportunities for its young officers. At the same time, there was work to do, and Ike got some of the most interesting assignments that were available.

In 1922 he was assigned to the Panama Canal Zone, where the army helped operate the great canal connecting the Atlantic and Pacific Oceans. There Ike met General Fox Conner, a man who influenced him enormously. General Conner prodded his young aide to take an interest in military history and strategy. He gave Ike books to read and quizzed him on them, discussing the great battles of history and how they had been won and lost. Ike later called his time with Fox

In 1903 the United States negotiated possession of a strip of land known as the Panama Canal Zone across the newly formed country of Panama. Between 1904 and 1914, it built a canal crossing the narrow isthmus of land between the Pacific Ocean and the Gulf of Mexico. The U.S. Army took a leading role in building the canal, and for many years U.S. soldiers were stationed there to protect its operation. The Canal Zone and the canal itself reverted to the government of Panama in 2000.

☆ ☆ ☆

Conner his "graduate school in military affairs and the humanities." General Conner also gave Eisenhower a piece of advice that would make a huge difference in his career. "Always take your job seriously, never yourself," Conner said.

In 1925 General Conner recommended Ike for the Command and General Staff School at Fort Leavenworth, Kansas. There Eisenhower began to develop his new interest in broad military questions. He proved able to master detail, to work under pressure, and to work well on a team. He finished first in a class of 275 officers. Because of his strong performance, he was chosen to write descriptions of the great battlefields of World War I for a history of great battlefields in U.S. military history. To accomplish this task, Ike and his family moved to Paris from July to November in 1928.

Eisenhower returned to Washington, where he became an aide to a military giant, General Douglas MacArthur. During World War I, MacArthur had become the youngest brigadier general in the history of the U.S. Army. In 1929 he was army chief of staff. MacArthur was a peacock of a man, always strutting and displaying his sharp mind and sense of authority. Ike learned much from MacArthur, yet he never viewed the older man as a model officer. In later years, Ike's style of leadership would provide a strong contrast to MacArthur's. He was more tolerant of people's differences and failings and was a keen student of human nature in a way MacArthur was not.

In 1935 Eisenhower was assigned to the Philippines. Once again he was an aide to General MacArthur, who served first as chief American adviser to the Philippine armed forces and later as their commander. In the Pacific and in other parts of the world, the clouds of war were gathering once again.

War Approaches

In the Pacific, Japan had become an aggressive new power, eager to gain new territories and resources. In 1931 it seized the mineral-rich region of Manchuria from China, beginning a long period of war in Asia. In Europe, the dictator Adolf Hitler took power in Germany in 1933. Soon he had broken Germany's treaty promises not to rebuild its armies. In 1935 still another dictator, Benito Mussolini

General Douglas MacArthur and his second in command, Colonel Dwight Eisenhower, in Washington in 1932.

of Italy, attacked and overran the African country of Ethiopia, making it an Italian colony. Soon these three powers would agree to cooperate in their drive for world domination.

By 1938 Hitler's Germany was threatening its neighbors. Great Britain and France, eager to avoid another war, refused to take firm action. Germany took over Austria, then Czechoslovakia. Finally, in 1939, it set its sights on Poland. On September 1, 1939, German armies marched across the Polish border. Within days, Great Britain and France declared war. The conflict that would be known as World War II had begun. Dwight Eisenhower would have an important role to play in its outcome.

Chapter 3

Headed for Leadership ——————————

Through 1940 and early 1941, Americans still hoped that somehow they could stay out of the growing war. Yet by June 1941, Germany had occupied nearly all of Western Europe and was carrying on a merciless bombing campaign against British cities. Late in June, it attacked the Soviet Union (the huge country that included present-day Russia and more than a dozen smaller republics that are now independent countries).

In the United States, President Franklin Roosevelt was working feverishly to make sure that the country was prepared for war in case it was forced to fight. As a part of the drive for preparedness, Dwight Eisenhower was asked to conduct huge *war games* in Louisiana to test new military equipment and strategies. These military maneuvers were a great success even though the army still lacked important war supplies. Ike's leadership gained him promotion to the temporary rank of brigadier general.

In December 1941, Ike was completing his report on the war games when Japanese bombers staged a surprise attack on the U.S. naval base at Pearl Harbor, in Hawaii. In a few hours, the attack destroyed or damaged much of the Pacific Fleet and cost the lives of more than 2,400 American servicemen. President Roosevelt called it "a date that will live in infamy," and asked Congress to declare war on Japan. Within days, the country was at war with Japan, Germany, and Italy.

Eisenhower was called to Washington to work as a planner in the War Department. After reviewing the worldwide situation, he concluded that Germany was the major enemy, even after Japan's attack on Pearl Harbor. In June 1942, he was named commanding general, European Theater of Operations. In this position, he would command not only American troops, but would be in overall command of all allied forces in Europe. He left Mamie in Washington, D.C., and headed for London.

The Glue That Holds the Allies Together ——

In some ways Ike was a curious choice to take on this responsibility. He had never been in combat; what he knew about fighting he had learned mostly in books and in the classroom. Yet President Roosevelt and Army Chief of Staff George C.

Japan's surprise attack on the U.S. military base at Pearl Harbor, Hawaii, killed 2,400 people and destroyed or damaged many ships and planes. The next day the United States declared war on Japan, becoming a combatant in World War II.

Marshall saw qualities in Eisenhower that they liked. He was smart, yet he was modest and open minded. He worked well with people, even difficult people. To succeed, he would need all of these skills and more.

The most difficult part of Ike's job was to deal diplomatically with advice from President Roosevelt and British prime minister Winston Churchill. Although the two men were friends, they often gave differing advice on managing the armed

Eisenhower with General George C. Marshall, the U.S. Army chief of staff who was the leading planner of U.S. strategy during the war. Eisenhower was his most trusted general in the field.

forces. A related problem was the friction between American and British soldiers. The British resented the recently arrived "Yanks," and the Americans suspected the "Brits" in return. Ike made it clear that he would never favor one side or the other and that he did not care who got the credit for successes. He only wanted to get the job done. His quiet but firm leadership helped keep the Allied forces working smoothly together.

Torch, Husky, and Avalanche

The Allied governments agreed that their first new offensive should be in North Africa. The plan, called Operation Torch, called for landing British and American troops in Morocco. This army, together with the British army in eastern North Africa, could trap the main German army between them. Operation Torch began under General Eisenhower's command in November 1942. Although there were setbacks and many casualties, the landings succeeded. The Allies, attacking from the east and the west, trapped German and Italian forces on the coast of Tunisia. On May 13, 1943, 240,000 Germans and Italians became prisoners of war.

The Allies' next objective was southern Europe. The target was the Italian island of Sicily, barely 100 miles (160 km) across the Mediterranean Sea from

Fast Facts
WORLD WAR II

Who: The Axis powers (Germany, Italy, and later Japan), opposed by the Allies (Britain, France, and the Soviet Union, and others, joined by the United States in December 1941, after Japan attacked Pearl Harbor in Hawaii

When: September 1939–August 1945

Where: In Europe, including the western Soviet Union; the Middle East and North Africa; China, Southeast Asia, and the Pacific islands; also on the seas in the Mediterranean Sea and the Atlantic, Pacific, and Indian Oceans

Why: The Axis powers invaded neighboring countries in search of territory, natural resources, and power. The Allied nations united to oppose the aggression of the Axis nations.

Outcome: The Allies took back lands occupied by the Axis powers, then invaded Italy and Germany and bombed Japan. Italy surrendered in 1943; Germany surrendered in May 1945 after its capital, Berlin, was occupied by Soviet troops; Japan surrendered in August 1945 after U.S. planes dropped atomic bombs on the cities of Hiroshima and Nagasaki.

Troops under Eisenhower's command first saw combat in the deserts of North Africa. Here they are dug in on a ridge at Kasserine Pass in Tunisia in 1943.

Tunisia. This joint British-American mission, called Operation Husky, began on July 9, 1943. Ike worked to coordinate the British and American attacks, but he had to struggle with two difficult leaders. U.S. general George S. Patton was a brilliant leader and a student of military history, but he was willful and proud. British field marshal Bernard Montgomery was also effective but difficult. When their forces reached Sicily, Patton and Montgomery raced each other to the objective, competing for headlines and credit. Ike scolded both men often, reminding them that the campaign was a team effort. They obeyed his orders, but never cooperated fully. Still, the Allies drove the enemy from Sicily by August 17.

The code name for the attack on the Italian mainland was Operation Avalanche. It began well with the capture of Naples on September 9, but progress in capturing the remainder of the Italian peninsula was slow and costly.

Overlord

In November 1943, the leaders of the most powerful Allied nations—President Franklin Roosevelt of the United States, Prime Minister Winston Churchill of Great Britain, and Premier Joseph Stalin of the Soviet Union—met in Tehran, Iran. There they agreed that the Allies in Western Europe would invade enemy-occupied France in the spring of 1944. Preliminary planning had already begun. In December, General Eisenhower was named supreme commander of Allied Expeditionary Forces. After a brief visit with Mamie in Washington, he returned to Britain to continue planning for the great invasion.

Code-named Overlord, the operation was certain to be dangerous. No army had ever landed so many men and so much equipment from the sea. If it failed, it would be a disaster for the Allied cause, but if it succeeded, it could fatally weaken the German armies, who were already defending against attackers from the east and the south. A third front would stretch their resources to the breaking point.

The Allies soon settled on a location for the attack, along the beaches of Normandy, about 100 miles (160 km) across the English Channel from staging areas in southern England. The final plan for Operation Overlord was one of the most elaborate ever devised. It involved thousands of ships and hundreds of thousands of men, including Canadian, Polish, Australian, and Free French units as well as Britons and Americans. Also involved were aircraft squadrons, gliders, and paratroopers, who would parachute behind enemy lines in the hours before the main landings.

The pressure on Ike was enormous. To relieve stress, he chain-smoked cigarettes throughout the months leading to the invasion. He seemed to live on sandwiches, coffee, and smoke. The choice of an invasion date involved careful calculations of the tides along the Normandy beaches. Then, as the chosen day drew near, Ike and his advisers watched the weather forecasts apprehensively. The English Channel was stormy almost year-round, and bad weather could defeat the Allied attack even before they reached the beaches. Finally, Ike set the attack for dawn on June 6, 1944.

General Eisenhower chats with troops hours before the D-Day invasion on June 6, 1944.

In the hours before the attack, Ike visited members of the 101st Airborne

Division of the U.S. Army. These paratroopers were to land behind enemy lines

before dawn, one of the most hazardous assignments on a very hazardous day. Ike

U.S. troops wade toward the beach under heavy enemy fire on D-Day.

knew he was asking a lot of them. Years later, when asked to name his greatest

moment as a military commander, he replied, "When I got word that the 82nd and

101st Airborne Divisions had landed on the Cherbourg Peninsula."

Success!

In the first hours of the gigantic invasion, hundreds of small things went wrong. Some landing craft were swamped by high waves. Some paratroopers landed in trees or in the middle of German-occupied villages. Thousands of brave invaders were killed on the beaches by German fire. Viewed from a broader perspective, however, the invasion went according to plan. Allied forces established footholds on the beaches, then doggedly drove inland, overpowering German positions.

Within a few days, huge shipments of supplies were arriving along the shore, and the great army began to drive German occupiers backward toward the German border. The D-Day invasion opened Europe to liberation. On August 25, less than 12 weeks after D-Day, Allied troops marched into Paris, the French capital, welcomed by cheering crowds.

The Bulge

By late 1944, German forces were retreating through France and Belgium in the west. As the Allies approached the border between Belgium and Germany, however, German resistance increased. On December 16, 1944, the Germans began a counteroffensive in the Ardennes, a forested region where the borders of France, Belgium, and Germany meet. Eisenhower ordered immediate reinforcements to the point of the attack, but the Germans still pushed a huge "bulge" into the Allied line, threatening to divide the Allied force in two.

Even as reports of losses and withdrawals continued, Ike refused to panic. He told his staff not to be downcast, pointing out that the counteroffensive could weaken the Germans and shorten the war. Once again, he called on his two trusty generals, Montgomery and Patton, to attack the bulge. They more than fulfilled his hopes. American and British forces, aided by the U.S. Air Force, blunted the German assault and soon turned the tables on the enemy. Ike later wrote, "Our men responded gallantly. . . . These were the times when grand strategy became a soldiers' war."

The Battle of the Bulge lasted for more than five weeks. *Casualties* (combatants killed, injured, or missing) were heavy, and surrounding towns were shattered. The Germans took heavy losses, and this proved to be their last major offensive of the war. Their failure to carry the day helped sap their strength and their will to fight.

War's End

Even as the Allies forced the German retreat, the United States received sad news. On April 12, 1945, President Franklin Roosevelt died. As one of the architects of Allied strategy during the war, he had made a huge contribution, but he did not

Eisenhower points out something to British field marshal Bernard Montgomery (right). Montgomery often disagreed with Eisenhower, who was the supreme commander of Allied forces in Western Europe.

survive to see the final victory. Hours after Roosevelt's death, Vice President Harry Truman was sworn in as president. He would be the nation's new commander in chief.

As British and American troops entered Germany from the west, Soviet troops were closing in from the east, approaching Berlin, the German capital. American and Soviet troops met along the Elbe River, about 70 miles (113 km) to the south of Berlin. As Soviet troops entered the city on April 30, 1945, Adolf Hitler killed himself in his underground bunker. A week later German military and civil authorities offered their unconditional surrender to Allied commanders at a schoolhouse in Rheims, France.

During his brief statement after the surrender, Ike did not smile or offer small talk. A reporter wrote, "Eisenhower was brief and terse as always. His voice was cold and hard. In a few clipped sentences he made it plain that Germany was a defeated nation and that henceforth all orders to the German people would come from the Allies. He said they would be obeyed."

The war in Europe was over. Huge crowds in Britain and America celebrated V-E (or Victory in Europe) Day. In the next few months, Eisenhower was transformed from an overburdened commander to a world hero. He was honored and cheered wherever he went, first in Great Britain and later in the United States.

Meanwhile, the war in the Pacific continued. By early August, U.S. troops had isolated the home islands of Japan. A massive invasion was planned to force Japan to surrender. Then on August 6, President Truman announced that the United States had exploded an atomic bomb of unimagined power over the

Eisenhower and Britain's Sir Arthur Tedder make solemn statements to the press after German authorities surrendered on May 7, 1945.

Eisenhower returns home in June 1945 to join Mamie and their son John, who had graduated from the U.S. Military Academy a year earlier.

Japanese city of Hiroshima. More than 70,000 people were killed instantly. When Japan did not immediately respond to demands for surrender, a second atom bomb was dropped over Nagasaki, Japan, on August 9. Finally, news of the Japanese surrender was announced early on August 14, which was celebrated as V-J Day (or Victory over Japan Day) around the world.

At long last, World War II was over.

The Challenges of Peace

President Truman appointed General Eisenhower as the new army chief of staff, replacing General George C. Marshall. This turned out to be one of the toughest jobs Eisenhower ever had and one of the most disagreeable. He had to oversee the rapid reduction of the American army from more than 8 million to a tiny fraction of that number. The rapid downsizing required the dismissal of many longtime army officers and reduced opportunities for those who remained.

Even though he disliked his job as chief of staff, Ike did enjoy the chance to relax and adjust to a more normal life after three intense years of military command. He and Mamie settled at Fort Meyer, just across the Potomac River from Washington. Their son, John Eisenhower, was an officer in the U.S. Army. He had graduated from the U.S. Military Academy on June 6, 1944, a day when his father had been busy commanding the D-Day invasion.

During his time as army chief of staff, Ike was part of a team that included General Marshall and others, advising President Truman on a new military strategy for the postwar years. With Germany defeated, concern quickly shifted to the Soviet Union, which was establishing Communist governments in the newly liberated countries of Eastern Europe. The new U.S. strategy was based on "containment" of the Soviets. This policy affirmed that no additional countries would fall under the rule of international Communism.

Time for a Change

By 1947, Eisenhower was eager to retire from the army and become a private citizen. He began to write his memoirs of the war years, *Crusade in Europe*. It was published in 1948, receiving widespread praise and strong sales. He considered becoming a gentleman farmer or the president of a small college. Then in 1948, he accepted the position as president of Columbia University—not a small college, but a prestigious university in New York City.

Eisenhower at a ceremony on the steps of Columbia University's library. He served as president of the university from 1948 to 1952.

Many of his friends had hoped that Ike would run for the presidency of the United States instead. He was the most admired man in the country, and his experience seemed to qualify him for the office. Democrats and Republicans each offered their party's nomination. When President Truman suggested he run as a Democrat, Ike reportedly replied, "God forbid."

Truman himself decided to run for a full term as president in 1948, and in a surprise he defeated Republican candidate Thomas E. Dewey of New York. In the meantime, Eisenhower settled in as a university president, where he emphasized connecting academic life to the real world. One program he established, the American Assembly, continues to further that goal today.

Serving His Country Again ————————

In 1950 a country tired of war was dragged back into combat. The Communist government of North Korea, with the support of the Soviet Union and a new Communist government in China, attacked South Korea. President Truman called on the United Nations to provide military support for the South Korean government. It agreed, and American troops were committed to defend South Korea, under the command of General Douglas MacArthur.

Later that year, President Truman asked Eisenhower to return to active military duty. The United States was organizing the North Atlantic Treaty Organization (NATO), an alliance of nations in Western Europe to defend against any future aggression by the Soviet Union. Truman asked Ike to become the first supreme commander of the alliance. His experience and his reputation among European leaders made him the best man for the job. Eisenhower readily agreed. He took a leave of absence from Columbia and moved with Mamie to Paris.

In Europe, Ike quickly sized up the problems of the alliance and its military forces. Using his diplomatic skills, he urged all parties to end their petty disagreements and work for a single goal. In a few short months, he helped shape the first NATO forces and gave them a new self-confidence. Even as he struggled to complete his work, he was in demand for a greater service.

Chapter 4

Politics Beckons

During the early 1950s the Republican party began discussing its candidate for the 1952 elections. The nation had been governed by a Democratic president for nearly 20 years, but there were signs that voters were ready for a change. The big question was who would make the strongest candidate.

Many Republicans favored Ohio's Robert A. Taft, a leader in the U.S. Senate, who was known as "Mr. Republican." Eisenhower knew Robert Taft and liked him personally, but disagreed with him about U.S. foreign policy. Taft favored withdrawing U.S. troops from overseas and did not favor military aid to U.S. allies in Europe. Ike felt that an American presence abroad was essential to preserving freedom and democracy there. He was especially forceful in supporting a strong U.S. alliance with the democracies of Europe.

Other Republicans shared Ike's views, and they became determined to draft the NATO commander as the party's presidential nominee. Many visited him in his headquarters near Paris, seeking to convince him that he must run for president. They knew that the popular war hero, with his calm manner and warm smile, would be a strong candidate against any Democratic opponent. No one else in the party had the same winning personality and record.

Ike listened to his visitors and asked many questions about the political scene, but he would not commit to run for president. "I have a job to do here," he told his visitors. He was careful *not* to say that he would turn down the nomination. He said only that he would not *run*. Pressure to run continued to build, however. In February 1952, his supporters staged a huge "Eisenhower for President" rally at Madison Square Garden in New York City. More than 15,000 supporters gathered to hear speeches supporting his candidacy and to wave signs that said "We Want Ike" and "We Like Ike." A film of the rally was flown to France so that Ike could see the enthusiasm for himself. When he saw the film, he broke into tears. He had not realized just how much he was admired.

His supporters also gained his permission to put his name on the ballot in the Republican presidential primary in New Hampshire. Ike did not return to the United States or campaign in any way, but in the March 14 vote he won a convincing victory over Senator Taft. Two weeks later, Ike finally announced that he

After receiving the Republican nomination for president in 1952, Eisenhower salutes the crowd with Mamie, vice-presidential candidate Richard Nixon, and Pat Nixon.

would be a candidate for president and that he would resign as commander of NATO effective June 1. At the Republican convention in July, Eisenhower won the Republican nomination on the first ballot. Following the advice of party leaders, he chose 39-year-old Richard Nixon, a senator from California, as his running mate.

The Crusade

At the convention Ike promised a "crusade" for better government. He said he would be more aggressive in confronting Communist nations abroad, that he would end the long expansion of the federal government, and that he would reduce government involvement in citizens' everyday lives. Drawing on values developed during his Kansas boyhood, he said that he wanted to make it possible for people to realize their ambitions based on their own hard work and personal ingenuity. He opposed a government that took too much of people's hard-earned income in taxes.

Campaigning across America by train, plane, and automobile that fall, Eisenhower sharply criticized the policies of the Truman administration. Truman himself had decided not to run for another term, but he campaigned actively for the Democratic nominee, Illinois governor Adlai Stevenson. Stevenson was a strong supporter of Democratic policies during the past 20 years. Republicans made a simple distinction between the candidates, pointing out that Ike stood for less government while Stevenson supported more government.

The Republican campaign in 1952 was reduced to a simple formula—C_2K_1, which stood for "Communism, Corruption, and Korea." "Communism" played on fears of Communists at home. It had been revealed that Communist spies stole U.S. nuclear secrets in the 1940s and delivered them to the Soviet Union. "Corruption" pointed to evidence that close political allies of President Truman had been profiting personally from government jobs by selling government favors. "Korea" referred to the war that had been raging there since mid-1950. Thousands of U.S. troops were committed there, and there seemed to be no end in sight. In October, Ike promised to visit Korea for himself to see the situation and to find an honorable end to the fighting.

Eisenhower's catchy campaign slogan used the nickname he had had since boyhood.

Americans watched as Ike crisscrossed the country, speaking in large cities and small hamlets in a whirlwind campaign that covered more than 50,000 miles (80,000 km). Although Ike was not as smooth a speaker as Governor Stevenson, he connected well with average people. They liked his straightforward talk and his stories about the need to keep prices down and restore the dollar's buying power. In addition, Ike's experience as a military leader spoke volumes. Americans would be safe under the leadership of Dwight D. Eisenhower.

When Americans voted in November 1952, they gave Ike a landslide victory. He won 39 of the 48 states, even carrying Texas, Florida, Virginia, and Tennessee in the South, which had long been solidly Democratic. He also helped elect Republican majorities in Congress.

An Honorable Truce in Korea

Ike did not wait to be sworn in as president to visit Korea. He visited the embattled country in December 1952 and quickly concluded that the United States would have to accept a less-than-complete victory. The fighting was then going on near the prewar border between North and South Korea. Ike's negotiators battled for a settlement that assured South Korea would not lose any territory to the Communist aggressors from the North. Ike also let it be known that if Communist nations insisted on continuing the fight, he would consider the use of nuclear weapons.

By mid-1953, an *armistice* was signed. Both parties committed to end the fighting and to create a demilitarized zone separating the two countries. It ran very near the earlier border. Even though the fighting ended, no real peace treaty between North and South Korea was signed. The United States stationed troops in South Korea for more than 50 years to guard against another outbreak.

President-elect Eisenhower visits troops in Korea during a visit in December 1952. He soon brought the Korean War to a negotiated settlement.

Dealing With the Russians

The nation's major worry in 1953 remained the possibility of a nuclear war with the Soviet Union. The Soviets had detonated their first atomic bomb in 1949 and were known to be working on a more powerful hydrogen bomb similar to the one recently tested by the United States.

Then in March 1953, the Soviet leader Joseph Stalin died after ruling with an iron hand for 24 years. What kind of policy would the new leaders follow? A wave of apprehension swept the world. On April 16, President Eisenhower addressed the change in a nationally televised speech. It was called "A Chance for Peace." He condemned the competition between the United States and the Soviets to build more and bigger weapons and suggested peaceful uses for the huge amounts of money that went into the arms race. He expressed the willingness of the United States to limit spending for armaments if the Soviets would do the same.

Later in 1953, in a speech at the United Nations, Eisenhower explained that the United States wanted to share what it knew about atomic energy with the rest of the world, for the good of all mankind. In this "Atoms for Peace" speech, he pointed out that atomic energy could improve people's lives in many ways, providing inexpensive electricity and new tools to improve health. Ike wanted citizens of all nations to benefit from atomic energy, not just the United States.

The new leaders of the Soviet Union did not respond to the president's invitations, and his hopes for arms limitation and cooperation in developing peaceful uses for nuclear power were not realized. Still, the president's deep concern for peace established the groundwork for negotiations by later presidents with the Soviet Union.

The Senator and the President

During the first years of his presidency, Eisenhower's main problems seemed to be not with the Soviets or with Democrats in Congress, but with fellow Republicans. Republican senator Joseph R. McCarthy of Wisconsin led a small group of militant anti-Communists who gained nationwide attention for their investigations of supposed Communists in the government. McCarthy claimed that the president was not doing enough to identify and prosecute such traitors.

McCarthy used false and exaggerated charges to alarm the public. Ike came to believe that McCarthy was interested only in promoting himself. The president had a program to weed out government workers he called "security risks," but McCarthy kept attacking him for being "soft on Communism."

Anti-Communist crusader Joseph McCarthy.

The problem was finding an effective way to end McCarthy's scare tactics. If the president denounced him, the senator would charge that Eisenhower himself "has something to hide." In addition, the senators would probably back one of their own members. "The Senate is a club," Eisenhower reminded one of his friends. He decided to ignore Senator McCarthy publicly, but to speak out in favor of protecting Americans' civil liberties and against all who threatened these liberties.

During the fall of 1953, McCarthy attacked leaders of the U.S. Army for supposedly allowing Communists to gain promotions and influence. These charges angered the president, who knew there was no truth to them. He began working behind the scenes to curb McCarthy's power. Finally in 1954, the Senate itself began an investigation of McCarthy and his methods. That December, it *censured* Senator McCarthy. This formal rebuke helped end his power, and his investigations came to a close.

Productive Years

Eisenhower felt confident advocating a "middle way" in American politics, a path between those who wanted what he thought was too much government, and those who wanted too little. During his first term, he reduced federal taxes and helped streamline government processes, cutting "red tape" so that government offices worked more efficiently.

The president went to bat for two major new government projects. The first was the Saint Lawrence Seaway, a joint project with Canada to improve the Saint Lawrence River, which connects the five Great Lakes to the Atlantic Ocean. When the project was completed, large seagoing vessels could sail up the Saint Lawrence and visit such new U.S. seaports as Buffalo, Cleveland, Detroit, and Chicago. The seaway was especially useful for shipping iron ore, wheat, and other bulky cargo.

In 1955 Eisenhower proposed a major new interstate highway system to be financed largely by the federal government through gasoline taxes. Recalling the painfully slow cross-county military convoy in 1919, he argued that an improved new system of highways was important for national defense as well as personal travel and truck transport. The Germans had been pioneers of the high-speed expressway, the *autobahn*, before World War II. Recalling those well-

During the 1950s millions of new homes were built in suburbs across the country. Many were bought by World War II veterans with the help of government-guaranteed loans.

designed highways, Ike insisted that the new interstate highways have multiple lanes and ramps by which cars could enter or leave the highway without slowing the flow of traffic. The interstate system was built over the next 40 years. At its completion in the 1990s, it contained more than 40,000 miles (64,000 km) of highway.

The president was able to propose such new spending because the nation was enjoying prosperous times, and most citizens shared his optimistic spirit. Employment was high, and millions of people were moving from cities to single-family homes in the suburbs. Nearly every home had a television set, and more families than ever before owned one or more cars. Not surprisingly, when these families considered how good economic conditions were, they gave a lot of credit to President Eisenhower.

Rights for African Americans

In 1953, his first year in office, President Eisenhower appointed Earl Warren, then governor of California, as Chief Justice of the United States. As the presiding officer of the Supreme Court, Warren played a major role in extending *civil rights* to African Americans. In 1954 the court ruled unanimously that racial segregation in public schools was unconstitutional. This landmark ruling, *Brown* v. *Board of Education of Topeka*, sparked a period of increased activism among African Americans, who began to test segregation laws throughout the South. It also caused a backlash from white citizens who favored segregation.

The president himself made no comment on the Supreme Court ruling, causing some to question his support for protecting civil rights. His record on the issue was mixed. As army chief of staff, he had supervised the integration of all units in the army (before, soldiers served in all-white or all-black units). As president, he appointed E. Frederic Morrow, the first African American to serve as an adviser on a president's staff. He also ended segregation of public facilities such as restaurants and theaters in Washington, D.C. Even so, Eisenhower seemed reluctant to take a public stand on civil rights. He had little to say in public about the oppression and unfairness African Americans faced in their everyday lives. Privately, he expressed the belief that improvement in relations between white and black Americans would depend on a gradual change in people's "hearts and minds."

The Heart Attack

When Eisenhower took office at 62, he was the oldest first-term president since James Buchanan in 1857. He kept a busy schedule as president, but he also found time for recreation. His main exercise was playing golf, which he did as often as his schedule and the weather allowed.

Then, during a vacation in Denver in September 1955, he suffered a serious heart attack. The president's illness was big news around the country and the world. People suddenly realized how much they liked him and were depending on him. Ike's doctors made him take a long rest and encouraged him to give his assistants more responsibility in running the government. Ike spent a good deal of his recovery time on the farm he and Mamie had bought in Gettysburg,

Eisenhower and his medical team at Fitzsimmons Army Hospital near Denver, Colorado, in 1955. He was recovering from a heart attack.

Pennsylvania. It was close enough to Washington so that his cabinet and other political leaders could attend meetings there. Only after Christmas did Ike return to work full-time.

In early 1956, the president announced his decision to run for another term. A part of him wanted to retire to his farm, but he agreed with his advisers that there was still much that needed to be done. There was also no other Republican with Ike's record and high popularity.

The president's supporters got another scare about his health late that spring, not long before the Republican convention. On June 7, a long-standing problem in his small intestine flared up, and he was rushed to the hospital for surgery. The operation was a success, but the president's recovery was slow. He remained in the hospital for three weeks, then continued to recuperate at his Gettysburg farm. Finally, on July 10, he met with his campaign team and assured them that he was nearly recovered and was planning to run for re-election in November. Republicans across the country breathed a sigh of relief.

Chapter 5

The Campaign of 1956 ———————

Despite his health scare, 1956 was a good year for the president. The country enjoyed peace and prosperity. "Everything," said one writer, "is booming except the guns." Once again, the Democratic nominee was former Illinois governor Adlai Stevenson. He campaigned energetically, hoping to suggest that the president might not be strong enough to serve. By election day, however, Stevenson seemed exhausted, and Eisenhower seemed healthy and rested.

World affairs interrupted the campaign in the final week when two crises broke out at the same time. In the Middle East, Egyptian premier Gamal Abdel Nasser took control of the Suez Canal. The canal, then privately owned, crosses Egyptian territory, connecting the Mediterranean Sea and the Indian Ocean. Three close U.S. allies—Great Britain, France, and Israel—took action to recapture the

Eisenhower enjoys a campaign dinner during his 1956 campaign. Mamie is trying out an "I Like Ike" eyeshade.

canal by force to return it to its private owners. Israel sent troops into Egypt on October 31, and Britain and France attacked days later.

The incident gave President Eisenhower an opportunity to demonstrate his command in foreign policy. Although U.S. relations with Egypt were cool, he had been opposed to any use of force to recapture the canal. He condemned the invasion as illegal and warned the U.S. allies to pull back. The administration also applied pressure through the United Nations. Finally, all three countries withdrew, ending a serious threat to peace in the Middle East.

Meanwhile, the people of Budapest, the capital city of Hungary, had risen up against the Soviet-controlled Hungarian government. On October 31, the Soviets sent army tanks into the city to put down the uprising. In the next few days as many as 30,000 Hungarians were killed as the Soviets restored order by force. This was a more difficult situation for Eisenhower and the United States. Ike praised the Hungarian freedom fighters, but he realized that Western nations could not take military action in Hungary without risking a nuclear war with the Soviets. In the following months he did make it easier for freedom fighters who escaped from Hungary to settle in the United States.

On November 6, 1956, Americans voters re-elected Eisenhower by a landslide. This time he won all but six states. Millions of new voters liked Ike, as did suburban voters, rural voters, and a surprising percentage of people who lived in cities and traditionally voted for the Democrats. They voted for Ike partly because of who he was, partly because he had delivered on his promises. They felt safer and more optimistic about the state of the country under Eisenhower's firm leadership.

...y continued its strong performance in 1957. Sales of new autos ... set new records. Yet two events that fall reminded Americans ...an faced serious challenges both overseas and at home.

Both the United States and the Soviet Union were working feverishly on rockets. The main purpose for such rockets was military—they could be used to deliver weapons thousands of miles. Both nations realized, however, that rockets might also have scientific uses. Both were at work on the idea of sending a man-made *satellite* into orbit around Earth. Many people believed that this was beyond human capabilities. Then on October 4, 1957, the Soviets announced that they had launched a small satellite called Sputnik into orbit. The tiny object was sending radio signals confirming that it was circling Earth every few hours. The announcement caused a worldwide sensation.

In the United States, amazement was combined with alarm. It was a shock that this accomplishment was achieved first by the Soviets and not by Americans. Were we behind the Soviets in rocketry? What must we do to keep up? President Eisenhower assured citizens that Sputnik was nothing to worry about and that U.S. technology remained the best in the world, but not everyone was convinced. Doubts increased in 1958, when highly publicized U.S. efforts to put a satellite into orbit failed. One exploded on the launching pad, and another fell harmlessly into the ocean. Newspapers called the American satellites "Kaputnik," "Dudnik," and "Flopnik."

The launch of Sputnik began the "space race," which would continue for many years as American and Soviet programs competed to send men into orbit, then to the moon. The most immediate effect of Sputnik, however, was that Congress made large appropriations to improve the teaching of science and mathematics in American schools.

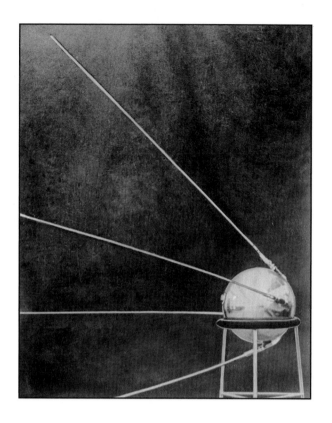

Sputnik was launched by the Soviet Union in October 1957. It was the first man-made satellite to be put into orbit around Earth. Americans were shocked that the Soviets accomplished this feat before the United States.

Eisenhower agreed that improving education could help Americans maintain their dominance in world affairs.

The Crisis at Little Rock

Even before Eisenhower's re-election, the growing campaign by African Americans to gain civil rights protection was gaining national attention. In December 1955, black citizens in Montgomery, Alabama, protested against segregation laws that forced African Americans to sit in special sections on city buses. The Reverend Martin Luther King Jr. directed a *boycott* of the buses and white-owned stores. African Americans refused to ride the buses or shop at the white-owned stores until segregation on buses was ended. The boycott continued for nearly a year, and the city finally agreed to end segregation on buses.

Meanwhile, a wave of violence against African Americans was sweeping Mississippi. In 1955 several African Americans were killed after they tried to vote in local elections, and no one was prosecuted for their deaths. In another case, 14-year-old Emmett Till was kidnapped and killed after he was accused of whistling at a white woman.

To address the growing conflict, Eisenhower's attorney general, Herbert Brownell, drafted a civil rights bill to establish and protect the right of African Americans to vote. Only a small handful of Southern blacks ever voted. The majority were kept away by difficult literacy tests (no tests were given to whites) or by steep poll taxes. Many others were too afraid of white retaliation to vote.

No civil rights bill had been passed in Congress since 1875, and many observers doubted that the Eisenhower bill would pass. It received broad support in the House of Representatives but stalled in the Senate, where a group of powerful Southern Democrats refused to bring it to a vote. The Democratic majority leader, Lyndon B. Johnson of Texas, took on the job of persuading them. He

Lyndon B. Johnson

Democrat Lyndon Johnson played a major role in securing the passage of Eisenhower's Civil Rights Act. Three years later, Johnson was elected vice president with President John F. Kennedy. In 1963, when Kennedy died in office, Johnson became president. In his first two years in office, he succeeded in passing the Civil Rights Act of 1964, which strengthened the 1957 act, and the Voting Rights Act of 1965.

☆ ★ ☆

allowed the senators to amend the bill, making it more difficult to prosecute Southern election officials. Then he worked feverishly to gain a majority for the weakened bill. Finally, the watered-down version passed in the Senate. President Eisenhower signed it into law on September 9, 1957. It was not everything its supporters had hoped, but it paved the way for stronger civil rights legislation in coming years.

That same week the president faced another civil rights challenge. A federal court required all-white Central High School, in Little Rock, Arkansas, to admit a group of African American students. As the day approached, Arkansas governor Orval Faubus ordered out state National Guard troops to keep order around the school. When the black students arrived, the guardsmen refused to let them enter the school.

President Eisenhower met with Governor Faubus personally and explained that the federal court order had to be obeyed. Faubus seemed to agree, but when he went back to Arkansas he continued to resist. The next time the black students tried to enroll, white crowds around the school rioted, and Governor Faubus took no action. This made Ike angry. He believed that Faubus had lied to his face when promising to enforce the court order.

National Guard troops escort African American students into Central High School in Little Rock, Arkansas. Eisenhower ordered the troops to Little Rock when local officials refused to enforce a court order desegregating the school.

The president ordered 1,000 paratroopers from the 101st Airborne Division to Little Rock, and he put the state National Guard under federal command. Federal troops escorted the blacks students into the school, and they were allowed to enroll. Ike's forceful actions ended the crisis. In the future, the federal government would continue to support the desegregation of public schools. In the next few years, the schools in Little Rock and other cities in the South were integrated.

Two New States

Ever since the end of World War II, residents of Alaska and Hawaii, both U.S. territories, had been asking the U.S. government for statehood. Both territories played important roles in the war. The attack that brought the United States into the war occurred at Pearl Harbor, in Hawaii. The only sustained fighting on U.S. soil between U.S. and Japanese troops occurred in Alaska's Aleutian Islands. The territories served as important military posts during the war, and they continued to have strategic importance during the Cold War.

By 1958 Congress was considering a statehood bill that would admit both territories. Final approval for Alaska came late that year, and the president approved its admission as the 49th state on January 3, 1959. On August 21, Eisenhower proclaimed Hawaii the 50th state in the Union. Late in his term, he would visit both new states.

The States During the Presidency of Dwight D. Eisenhower

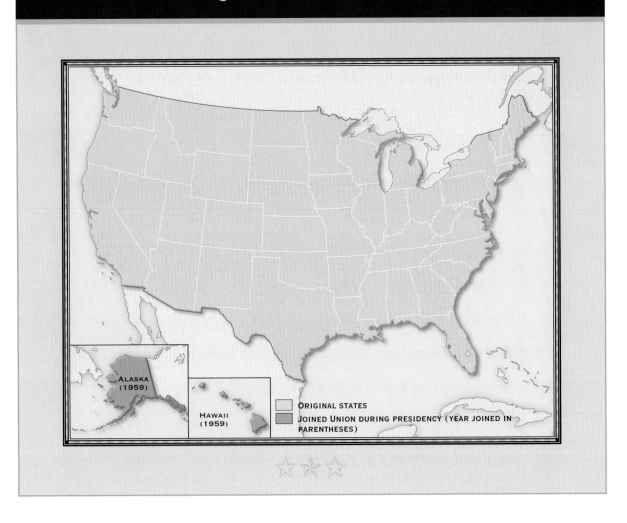

ALASKA
(1959)

HAWAII
(1959)

ORIGINAL STATES

JOINED UNION DURING PRESIDENCY (YEAR JOINED IN
PARENTHESES)

Waging Peace

The thing that mattered most to President Eisenhower was ensuring that there would never be a World War III. On one hand, he realized that the United States must remain strong to discourage its enemies. On the other hand, he continued to emphasize his willingness to ease tensions and find new ways to cooperate with other nations in creating a secure and peaceful world. In 1959 and 1960, he traveled around the globe, carrying the message that the United States was committed to peace. In December 1959, he visited ten nations in Europe, Asia, and North Africa. He was greeted by huge enthusiastic crowds. At one stop in India, a million people turned out. In 1960 he toured Latin America, where he was received with cheers. His last tour included stops in the Far East.

The president also played host to other world leaders. In 1959 Soviet premier Nikita Khrushchev spent two weeks in the United States. Eisenhower met with him informally on his Gettysburg farm to discuss reducing tensions between the two superpowers. Khrushchev toured the country, spending time on an Iowa farm and visiting California. Pleased with his visit and comfortable with the president, Khrushchev invited Ike and his grandchildren to visit Moscow in the spring of 1960.

Soviet premier Nikita Khrushchev presents President Eisenhower with a replica of a Soviet satellite during his visit to the United States in September 1959.

The U-2

Ike's visit to Moscow never took place. Weeks before the scheduled trip, on May 1, 1960, the Soviets shot down a high-altitude U.S. spy plane flying above its territory. Eisenhower had approved flights of secret U-2 spy planes to gather information on Soviet military bases and nuclear sites. He knew that the Soviets might shoot down one of the planes but felt that the information being gathered was worth the risk.

When the plane was first reported missing, U.S. officials assumed that the plane had crashed and the pilot, Francis Gary Powers, had been killed. Then the Soviets unveiled a nasty surprise. After the plane was hit by Soviet fire, Powers had parachuted out of his plane safely and was captured. The Soviets also recovered the wreckage of the plane. Premier Khrushchev criticized the United States for its "aggressive provocation." He said that he was insulted by the spying on his country and sharply criticized President Eisenhower. He withdrew his invitation to Eisenhower to visit Moscow. In mid-May, during a meeting of world leaders in Paris, Khrushchev refused to negotiate with Eisenhower. The U-2 crisis embarrassed the United States and ended Eisenhower's efforts to reduce tensions with the Soviet Union.

The Election of 1960

Eisenhower was the first president to be prohibited from running for a third term by the 22nd Amendment to the Constitution. The favorite for the Republican nomination was Vice President Richard Nixon. Eisenhower endorsed his vice president early in 1960, but did not take an active role in the campaign. The Democrats nominated Massachusetts senator John F. Kennedy.

Nixon was the early favorite, but Kennedy proved to be a strong campaigner and an attractive candidate. In the first televised debate between presidential candidates, Kennedy impressed many voters, while Nixon seemed pale and ill at ease. Kennedy took a lead in the opinion polls.

Finally in October, Eisenhower took a more active role. He rebutted Democratic attacks on his administration and pointed out Kennedy's lack of experience. By election night, the race was too close to call. When the votes were counted, John Kennedy was elected by a paper-thin margin. It was a heart-breaking defeat for Nixon and for the Republican party.

Days before leaving office, Eisenhower delivers his farewell address to the nation.

The Farewell Address

In his final days as president, Eisenhower asked for time on national television to address the nation. He might have recited all the good things that had happened during his eight years in office. Instead, he looked to the future. He warned that the world was still shadowed by the threat of war and the use of nuclear weapons. He confessed that he was disappointed not to have made more progress toward ending that threat. "I wish I could say tonight that a lasting peace is in sight," he said. "Happily, I can say that war has been avoided. But so much remains to be done."

The president also warned about the "military-industrial complex"—the growing influence of military planners and the huge defense industries that developed and built nuclear weapons, rockets, and other military hardware. "We must never let the weight of this combination endanger our liberties or democratic processes," he said. He urged citizens to remain alert "so that security and liberty may prosper together."

These sober warnings, coming from a great military hero and a popular president, made a lasting impact.

Departure

On the morning of January 20, 1961, Ike met briefly in the White House with the incoming president, John F. Kennedy. At noon he attended Kennedy's inauguration. A large storm early that morning had blanketed the city with a foot of snow. By the time Kennedy took his oath of office, the day had become intensely sunny and windy.

After a farewell lunch with his cabinet and staff, Ike joined Mamie for the drive to Gettysburg. There they were greeted by an enthusiastic crowd and treated

Eisenhower greets incoming president John F. Kennedy on Kennedy's inauguration day in January 1961.

to a testimonial dinner. Ike looked forward to this new chapter in his life as a elder statesman.

Chapter 6

An Active Retirement ——————

Dwight Eisenhower was 70 years old when he left office, but he still had lots of energy and many plans. One of his goals was to write, both about his presidency and his growing-up years in Kansas. *White House Years*, about his presidency, came out in two volumes, in 1963 and 1965. The account of his early life was called *At Ease: Stories I Tell to Friends (1967)*.

The ex-president was pleased to be consulted from time to time by President Kennedy, who called to discuss world affairs during several moments of crisis. After Kennedy's death, the new president, Lyndon Johnson, also consulted with Ike on a regular basis. Even though Eisenhower had private doubts about Johnson's actions in the growing war in Vietnam, he urged the nation to support its commander in chief.

Eisenhower's Mount Vernon

The first U.S. president, George Washington, retired from office to his beloved farm at Mount Vernon. Like Washington, Ike took great pleasure in managing his property. "All my life, I wanted to own a piece of land and leave it in better condition than I found it," he told a friend.

Ike's farm produced wheat, hay, oats, barley, soybeans, and corn. The main enterprise, however, was raising Black Angus cattle. In partnership with several old friends, the former president established one of Pennsylvania's leading "show cattle" farms. Ike's favorite bull, Ankonian 3551, won many prizes. So did other cattle in the Eisenhower herd, which at its peak numbered about a hundred animals.

Mamie enjoyed having a home of her own at long last. She supervised the decoration of the house, and devoted her energy to household duties. She enjoyed hunting for bargains at local stores. The best part of Ike's day was his evening time with Mamie. Sometimes he barbecued on an outdoor grill. Often, the Eisenhowers would eat their meals on TV tables while watching the news or a game show. Some nights Ike would spend time in his studio painting. Painting landscapes and portraits had long been one of his more relaxing hobbies.

Because he was naturally friendly, Ike met many local people and tourists when he was in town shopping. Some simply shouted, "Hello, Ike," from their

The Eisenhower farm in Gettysburg, Pennsylvania, included comfortable living quarters for Ike and Mamie during their retirement.

cars, while others wanted to shake his hand or ask for his autograph. Sometimes these encounters with strangers could be annoying, but Ike always took interruptions in stride. "Suppose people didn't like us," he once said. "That would be terrible, wouldn't it?"

Ike enjoyed his freedom but he had to learn how to adjust to civilian life after years as a military officer and president. He had never dialed a telephone, relying on assistants to reach people he wanted to talk to. His son John showed him how to dial numbers for himself. Ike also was not a very good driver, since others had driven him around for decades. "He would lean on the horn and 'gun'

Eisenhower at the easel, painting a landscape. Painting was one of his favorite hobbies.

the motor," John once recalled. Finally, Ike sometimes forgot to carry cash to pay for items in local stores. One of his assistants would have to pay for the items himself or arrange for the store to send a bill.

Ike at Work

On weekday mornings, Eisenhower usually arrived at his office on the Gettysburg College campus by 8 a.m. There he worked on his books, answered his mail, and greeted visitors. Gradually, he learned that he was no longer required to work long hours every day. When the weather was good, he would sneak out in the afternoon to play nine holes of golf. Even into his seventies Ike was a good golfer. He always practiced before going onto the course, and he made little small talk while playing. If he had a bad game, "he got pretty upset about it," his caddy recalled. In 1968 he scored his first hole in one, one of his proudest achievements as a golfer. Ike never lost his zest for winning.

Like many retirees, the Eisenhowers also enjoyed travel. In June 1964, they visited the beaches of Normandy to observe the 20th anniversary of the D-Day invasion. During the winters, they learned to escape the cold weather in Gettysburg by spending a few months in Palm Desert, California. There Ike could play golf as often as he wished.

All told, it was a busy life, so much so that Ike once noted that "retirement" was a strange word to describe his life. "I think I've had more demands made on me than I've ever had in my life," he told a reporter. The truth is that former presidents never fully retire.

The Final Years ———————————————

In 1965 Eisenhower celebrated his 75th birthday. Mamie made sure the occasion was a special one. A month later he suffered a serious heart attack. Ike had dealt with health problems before, but nothing this alarming. He realized that he needed to think about winding up some of his affairs. He told his herdsman at the farm to begin selling his cattle. It was time, as he told a friend, to "tidy up my affairs somewhat."

For another two years the Eisenhowers lived a normal life in Gettysburg, spending time with friends and family. Ike's book about growing up in Kansas, *At Ease: Stories I Tell to Friends*, was a national best seller in 1967. He began work almost immediately on a new book, a picture history of his life.

In April 1968, as Eisenhower was preparing to return from California to Gettysburg, he suffered another heart attack. Soon he was confined to a room at Walter Reed Army Hospital in Washington, where he spent the last year of his life. Mamie shared the hospital suite with him. Many visitors came to visit and chat with the former president, who continued to take an interest in world and national affairs.

One of Ike's special visitors was Richard Nixon, who was elected president in November 1968. Weeks later, Nixon's daughter Julie married Eisenhower's grandson David, uniting the two families. This gave the old president a lift even as his health continued to fail. Dwight Eisenhower watched Nixon's inauguration as president on television in January 1969. Two months later, on March 28, 1969, his heart failed. "I want to go," he told his family. "God take me."

Eisenhower the Man

Dwight Eisenhower was a modest man who achieved great things. Born in the horse-and-buggy age, he lived through an era of remarkable change. During his youth, automobiles and airplanes made their first appearance. By the time he died in 1969, men were about to walk on the moon.

Eisenhower took great changes in stride, but he also stood by values he had learned as a child. He believed that such values as hard work, honesty, and thrift remained good for all times. As president he tried to put these values into practice. He believed that governments, like individuals, should spend money they actually have rather than borrow. He was suspicious of big government and believed that the more it got involved in people's daily lives, the less they would be able to think and act for themselves.

Eisenhower was optimistic and forward-looking. Even though he recognized the dangers of the world situation during his presidency, he spent much of

President Dwight D. Eisenhower.

his energy working to bring a relaxation of tensions, reduction of armaments, and world peace. Because he had spent much of his life as a soldier, he had seen the ravages of war. This experience gave him a sense of urgency in seeking positive and peaceful solutions around the world.

As a general and as a president, Ike was a strong leader. As a young man, he had been a successful football coach. As a military and political leader, he applied his coaching techniques to leading. He gave his soldiers and his staff his trust and confidence. He treated them well, and made it clear that he was not interested in taking the credit for good ideas. Rather, he was interested in having the ideas work. As a result, his soldiers and his staff gave him their loyalty and did their best.

Eisenhower's Legacy ──────────────

What did Dwight Eisenhower accomplish as president?

Eisenhower himself was proud of changing the country's mood and outlook. "When I came to the presidency, the country was in an unhappy state," he said near the end of his life. "There was bitterness and there was quarreling. I tried to create an atmosphere of greater serenity and mutual confidence, and I think that over those eight years that was brought about." His optimism and competence eased the country's fears about Communists at home and the possibility of nuclear war. The country had a chance to catch its breath after the struggles of World War II.

Even as he calmed the country's fears, Eisenhower kept America strong. During his years as president, the country greatly increased its arsenal of nuclear weapons—in the hope that they would discourage enemies from hostile actions and would never have to be used. He hated the prospect of a nuclear war, but understood that military strength made it easier to keep the peace.

Eisenhower also contributed to the civil rights revolution. Supreme Court justices he appointed ordered the desegregation of public schools in 1954. During his second term, his administration proposed and helped to enact the first new Civil Rights Act since 1875. Finally, the president upheld school desegregation by sending federal troops to escort African American students into Central High School in Little Rock, Arkansas.

The Eisenhower administration also presided over a period of great prosperity and economic progress. The president aided the growing economy by sponsoring construction of the interstate highway system, which would bring new development to isolated areas across the country. His economic policies encouraged business by keeping inflation and taxes low.

When he died in 1969, Americans mourned Dwight D. Eisenhower as a fallen hero, but they also celebrated his life and accomplishments. His story

At the U.S. Military Academy, Eisenhower's "Order of the Day" for June 6, 1944, appears on the pedestal that holds his statue. These were the most famous words he ever wrote.

began in modest circumstances, yet led to great heights. It demonstrated that America remained a land of opportunity. Most of all, Americans remembered Eisenhower as a man of goodwill, seeking always to bring the country together, not to divide it.

Fast Facts

Dwight David Eisenhower

Birth:	October 14, 1890
Birthplace:	Denison, Texas
Parents:	David Jacob Eisenhower and Ida Stover Eisenhower
Brothers:	Arthur Bradford (1886–1958)
	Edgar Newton (1889–1971)
	Roy J. (1892–1942)
	Paul Dawson (1894–1895)
	Earl Dewey (1898–1968)
	Milton Stover (1899–1985)
Education:	United States Military Academy, graduated 1915
Occupation:	Career officer, United States Army
Marriage:	To Mamie Geneva Doud, July 1, 1916, at Denver, Colorado
Children:	(see First Lady Fast Facts, next page)
Political Party:	Republican
Public Offices:	34th President of the United States (1953–1961)
His Vice President:	Richard M. Nixon (1953–1961)
Major Actions as President:	1953 Delivers "A Chance for Peace" speech
	1953 Approves armistice ending fighting in Korea
	1956 Helps force withdrawal of British, French, and Israelis in Suez Canal crisis
	1957 Signs first Civil Rights Act since 1875; sends troops to Little Rock to enforce desegregation of Central High School
	1959 Signs bills admitting Alaska and Hawaii to statehood; hosts visit of Soviet premier Khrushchev
Death:	March 28, 1969, at Washington, D.C.
Age at Death:	78 years
Burial Place:	Eisenhower Center, Abilene, Kansas

Fast Facts

Mamie Geneva Doud Eisenhower

Birth:	November 14, 1896
Birthplace:	Boone, Iowa
Parents:	John Sheldon Doud and Elivera Carlson Doud
Sisters:	Eleanor
	Edna Mae
	Mabel Francis
Education:	East High School, Denver Colorado
	Wolcott School for Girls
Marriage:	To Dwight David Eisenhower, July 1, 1916, Denver, Colorado
Children:	Doud Dwight (Icky) (1917–1921)
	John Sheldon Doud (1922–)
Death:	November 1, 1979, at Washington, D.C.
Age at Death:	Nearly 83 years
Burial Place:	Eisenhower Center, Abilene, Kansas

Timeline

1890	1892	1909	1911	1915
David Dwight Eisenhower born October 14, in Denison, Texas.	Eisenhower family moves to Abilene, Kansas.	Eisenhower graduates from Abilene High School.	Enters U.S. Military Academy at West Point, New York.	Graduates from Military Academy, assigned to Fort Sam Houston, Texas.

1922	1925	1929	1935	1941
Eisenhower assigned to Panama as executive officer to General Fox Conner; son John S. D. Eisenhower born.	Attends Command and General Staff School, ranks first in class of 275 officers.	Serves as assistant to General Douglas MacArthur in Washington, D.C.	Serves in the Philippines, assisting General MacArthur in creating a Filipino army.	Plans successful military maneuvers in Louisiana.

1950	1952	1953	1956	1957
Returns to active military duty as supreme commander of NATO.	Wins Republican nomination for president, July; elected 34th president, November.	Approves armistice ending fighting in the Korean War.	Signs act beginning construction of the interstate highway system; re-elected to second term as president.	Signs Civil Rights Act of 1957; sends federal troops to enforce desegregation of high school in Little Rock, Arkansas.

1916	1917	1918	1919	1921
Marries Mamie Geneva Doud.	Son "Icky" born.	Eisenhower commands tank training at Camp Colt, Pennsylvania.	Joins Great Convoy, cross-country trek of military vehicles.	Icky dies of scarlet fever.

1942	1943	1944	1945	1948
Named commander, European Theater of Operations, June; directs North Africa landings, November.	Directs invasion of Sicily and Italian mainland; named supreme commander of Allied forces in Western Europe, December.	Directs invasion of France at Normandy as supreme Allied commander.	Germany surrenders, ending war in Europe, May; Japan surrenders, August; Eisenhower named army chief of staff, November.	Retires from army; appointed president of Columbia University.

1957	1959	1960	1961	1969
Russians launch Sputnik, first man-made satellite, into Earth orbit, October.	Eisenhower signs acts admitting Alaska and Hawaii as 49th and 50th states; hosts Soviet premier Nikita Khrushchev at Gettysburg.	American U-2 spy plane shot down over Soviet Union; Democrat John F. Kennedy defeats Republican Richard Nixon for presidency.	Eisenhowers move to their farm in Gettysburg, Pennsylvania.	Eisenhower dies March 28, 1969, is buried at the Eisenhower Center in Abilene, Kansas.

Glossary

armistice: an agreement to end fighting, usually until a formal peace treaty is negotiated and signed

autobahn: a German expressway, pioneered in the 1930s, with multiple lanes and ramps for entering and exiting

boycott: the refusal by a group to do business with its opponents until an objectionable rule or condition is changed

casualties: in a battle or campaign, a count of combatants killed, wounded, and missing

censure: a formal reprimand by a legislature or other official body to one of its members

civil rights: rights granted to all citizens, especially the right to equal treatment under the law

convoy: a group of military vehicles traveling together

influenza: a contagious disease often called "the flu"; severe influenza strains such as the one of 1918–1919 can cause thousands of deaths

pacifist: a person who opposes all wars

reparations: money damages paid by one country to another as a result of a treaty ending a war or dispute

satellite: a natural or man-made object that revolves around a larger object

war games: military exercises conducted by an armed service to test new strategies and equipment

Further Reading

Brenner, Samuel. *Dwight D. Eisenhower*. San Diego: Greenhaven Press, 2002.

Schultz, Randy. *Dwight D. Eisenhower*. Berkeley Heights, NJ: MyReportLinks.comBooks, 2003.

Young, Jeff C. *Dwight D. Eisenhower: Soldier and President*. Greensboro, NC: Morgan Reynolds, 2002.

MORE ADVANCED READING

Ambrose, Stephen E. *Dwight D. Eisenhower*. 2 volumes. New York: Simon & Schuster, 1983, 1984.

Eisenhower, Dwight D. *At Ease: Stories I Tell to Friends*. Garden City, NY: Doubleday, 1967.

———— *Crusade in Europe*. Paperback edition. Baltimore: Johns Hopkins University Press, 1997.

Eisenhower, Susan. *Mrs. Ike: Memories and Reflections on the Life of Mamie Eisenhower*. New York: Farrar, Straus and Giroux, 1996.

Parmet, Herbert S. *Eisenhower and the American Crusades*. New York: Macmillan, 1972.

Perret, Geoffrey. *Eisenhower*. New York: Random House, 1999.

Places to Visit

Eisenhower Birthplace
609 S. Lamar Avenue
Denison, TX 75020
(903) 465-8908

This State Historic Site centers on the house where Eisenhower was born in 1890. For further information, visit its Web site (address on following page).

The Dwight D. Eisenhower Library and Museum
200 Southeast Fourth Street
Abilene, KS 67410
(785) 263-6700
Toll-free: 1 (877) RING IKE

Located near Ike's boyhood home, the site includes that house the Eisenhower family lived in during the early 1900s. The museum offers exhibits on Ike's life and times. The library preserves documents from his presidential years.

Eisenhower National Historic Site
97 Taneytown Road
Gettysburg, PA 17325
Visitor Information: (717) 338-9114

The Eisenhower farm in Gettysburg is open to the public and offers special events during the year. The site is near the much larger Gettysburg Battlefield, which preserves the history of the Civil War battle fought there in 1863.

Online Sites of Interest

★ **Eisenhower Birthplace**

http://www.eisenhowerbirthplace.org/

The Web site of the state historic monument in Denison, Texas, where Ike was born in 1890. Offers features on his life.

★ **Eisenhower National Historic Site**

http://www.nps.gov/eise/

The Web site of the historic site on the Eisenhower farm in Gettysburg, Pennsylvania.

★ **Eisenhower Library and Museum**

http://www.eisenhower.archives.gov/

Provides a variety of information on Eisenhower's family, his military career, and his presidency.

★ **American Presidency**

http://www.americanpresident.org/history/dwighteisenhower/biography/

A useful biography of Eisenhower, which can be compared to biographies of other presidents at this site. Maintained by the Miller Center at the University of Virginia.

★ **IPL-POTUS**

http://www.ipl.org/div/potus/ddeisenhower.html

A brief summary of information on Eisenhower's presidency, provided by the University of Michigan School of Information. Includes links to other Eisenhower sites.

★ **U.S. Army Brochure**

http://www.army.mil/cmh-pg/brochures/ike/ike.htm

An informative summary of Ike's long career in the U.S. Army. Includes maps of military campaigns.

Table of Presidents

1. George Washington **2. John Adams** **3. Thomas Jefferson** **4. James Madison**

	1. George Washington	2. John Adams	3. Thomas Jefferson	4. James Madison
Took office	Apr 30 1789	Mar 4 1797	Mar 4 1801	Mar 4 1809
Left office	Mar 3 1797	Mar 3 1801	Mar 3 1809	Mar 3 1817
Birthplace	Westmoreland Co, VA	Braintree, MA	Shadwell, VA	Port Conway, VA
Birth date	Feb 22 1732	Oct 20 1735	Apr 13 1743	Mar 16 1751
Death date	Dec 14 1799	July 4 1826	July 4 1826	June 28 1836

9. William H. Harrison **10. John Tyler** **11. James K. Polk** **12. Zachary Taylor**

	9. William H. Harrison	10. John Tyler	11. James K. Polk	12. Zachary Taylor
Took office	Mar 4 1841	Apr 6 1841	Mar 4 1845	Mar 5 1849
Left office	**Apr 4 1841•**	Mar 3 1845	Mar 3 1849	**July 9 1850•**
Birthplace	Berkeley, VA	Greenway, VA	Mecklenburg Co, NC	Barboursville, VA
Birth date	Feb 9 1773	Mar 29 1790	Nov 2 1795	Nov 24 1784
Death date	Apr 4 1841	Jan 18 1862	June 15 1849	July 9 1850

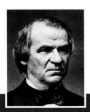   

17. Andrew Johnson **18. Ulysses S. Grant** **19. Rutherford B. Hayes** **20. James A. Garfield**

	17. Andrew Johnson	18. Ulysses S. Grant	19. Rutherford B. Hayes	20. James A. Garfield
Took office	Apr 15 1865	Mar 4 1869	Mar 5 1877	Mar 4 1881
Left office	Mar 3 1869	Mar 3 1877	Mar 3 1881	**Sept 19 1881•**
Birthplace	Raleigh, NC	Point Pleasant, OH	Delaware, OH	Orange, OH
Birth date	Dec 29 1808	Apr 27 1822	Oct 4 1822	Nov 19 1831
Death date	July 31 1875	July 23 1885	Jan 17 1893	Sept 19 1881

5. James Monroe

Mar 4 1817

Mar 3 1825

Westmoreland Co, VA

Apr 28 1758

July 4 1831

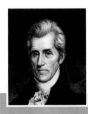

6. John Quincy Adams

Mar 4 1825

Mar 3 1829

Braintree, MA

July 11 1767

Feb 23 1848

7. Andrew Jackson

Mar 4 1829

Mar 3 1837

The Waxhaws, SC

Mar 15 1767

June 8 1845

8. Martin Van Buren

Mar 4 1837

Mar 3 1841

Kinderhook, NY

Dec 5 1782

July 24 1862

13. Millard Fillmore

July 9 1850

Mar 3 1853

Locke Township, NY

Jan 7 1800

Mar 8 1874

14. Franklin Pierce

Mar 4 1853

Mar 3 1857

Hillsborough, NH

Nov 23 1804

Oct 8 1869

15. James Buchanan

Mar 4 1857

Mar 3 1861

Cove Gap, PA

Apr 23 1791

June 1 1868

16. Abraham Lincoln

Mar 4 1861

Apr 15 1865•

Hardin Co, KY

Feb 12 1809

Apr 15 1865

21. Chester A. Arthur

Sept 19 1881

Mar 3 1885

Fairfield, VT

Oct 5 1829

Nov 18 1886

22. Grover Cleveland

Mar 4 1885

Mar 3 1889

Caldwell, NJ

Mar 18 1837

June 24 1908

23. Benjamin Harrison

Mar 4 1889

Mar 3 1893

North Bend, OH

Aug 20 1833

Mar 13 1901

24. Grover Cleveland

Mar 4 1893

Mar 3 1897

Caldwell, NJ

Mar 18 1837

June 24 1908

	25. William McKinley	**26. Theodore Roosevelt**	**27. William H. Taft**	**28. Woodrow Wilson**
Took office	Mar 4 1897	Sept 14 1901	Mar 4 1909	Mar 4 1913
Left office	**Sept 14 1901•**	Mar 3 1909	Mar 3 1913	Mar 3 1921
Birthplace	Niles, OH	New York, NY	Cincinnati, OH	Staunton, VA
Birth date	Jan 29 1843	Oct 27 1858	Sept 15 1857	Dec 28 1856
Death date	Sept 14 1901	Jan 6 1919	Mar 8 1930	Feb 3 1924

	33. Harry S. Truman	**34. Dwight D. Eisenhower**	**35. John F. Kennedy**	**36. Lyndon B. Johnson**
Took office	Apr 12 1945	Jan 20 1953	Jan 20 1961	Nov 22 1963
Left office	Jan 20 1953	Jan 20 1961	**Nov 22 1963•**	Jan 20 1969
Birthplace	Lamar, MO	Denison, TX	Brookline, MA	Johnson City, TX
Birth date	May 8 1884	Oct 14 1890	May 29 1917	Aug 27 1908
Death date	Dec 26 1972	Mar 28 1969	Nov 22 1963	Jan 22 1973

   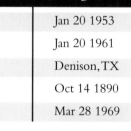  

	41. George Bush	**42. Bill Clinton**	**43. George W. Bush**	
Took office	Jan 20 1989	Jan 20 1993	Jan 20 2001	
Left office	Jan 20 1993	Jan 20 2001	—	
Birthplace	Milton, MA	Hope, AR	New Haven, CT	
Birth date	June 12 1924	Aug 19 1946	July 6 1946	
Death date	—	—	—	

29. Warren G. Harding

Mar 4 1921

Aug 2 1923•

Blooming Grove, OH

Nov 21 1865

Aug 2 1923

30. Calvin Coolidge

Aug 2 1923

Mar 3 1929

Plymouth, VT

July 4 1872

Jan 5 1933

31. Herbert Hoover

Mar 4 1929

Mar 3 1933

West Branch, IA

Aug 10 1874

Oct 20 1964

32. Franklin D. Roosevelt

Mar 4 1933

Apr 12 1945•

Hyde Park, NY

Jan 30 1882

Apr 12 1945

37. Richard M. Nixon

Jan 20 1969

Aug 9 1974★

Yorba Linda, CA

Jan 9 1913

Apr 22 1994

38. Gerald R. Ford

Aug 9 1974

Jan 20 1977

Omaha, NE

July 14 1913

—

39. Jimmy Carter

Jan 20 1977

Jan 20 1981

Plains, GA

Oct 1 1924

—

40. Ronald Reagan

Jan 20 1981

Jan 20 1989

Tampico, IL

Feb 6 1911

June 5 2004

• Indicates the president died while in office.
★ Richard Nixon resigned before his term expired.

Index

Page numbers in *italics* indicate illustrations.

About the Author

Michael J. Birkner is professor of history at Gettysburg College. A former editorial page editor at the *Concord Monitor* in New Hampshire, Birkner is author of many books and articles on 19th- and 20th-century American political history. He lives in Gettysburg, Pennsylvania, with his wife and three children.